Inspirations

Robert Diamond

Presentation by *BookLeaf Publishing*

Web: www.bookleafpub.com

E-mail: info@bookleafpub.com

ISBN: 9789357613231

First edition 2022

ACKNOWLEDGEMENT

I acknowledge that:

Everyone's unique and beautiful life, has meaning, has purpose. We can have more than one purpose.

Strive to look and go within to find yourself, your self worth, your self love and acceptance, your inner child, your masculine and feminine, your shadow and light, your soul, your spirit, your divinity, and make the connections. Embrace them, integrate them, love them, as you should unconditionally love and accept yourself.

Once you become centred and grounded as you connect with your self, you can be finally at peace and content in the knowing that you are of the divine, you are of the earth, and you have a truly unique and individual meaningful purpose, that is not bound by time or space and cannot be measured or compared against another's purpose, successes and challenges, but only by the peaceful easy feelings of happiness and joy, one will frequently experience by being on purpose.

Through constant personal development and self awareness will ones purpose come into view as you connect and fully amerce into the processes of the self and are willing and able to reflect and grow your infinite capacity to walk your path with purpose and through love.

The authentic, positive and pure beauty in this process has a magnitude of vibrational ripples which can shift and lift others to awaken to themselves, which will, in-turn generate phenomenal growth towards the collective consciousness and new paradigms.

Peace love recognition and support I send you all.

Sands of Time

It's you, my sweet lover, I see your smiling face,
And I, your man your lover, cherish our warm
embrace,

You and I,
side by side,
With the sands of time,
You and I, as we entwine
With the sands of time,

My heart, my sweet lover, beats strong for you
each day,
And your heart,my sweet lover, always I will
praise,
You and I,
side by side,
With the sands of time,
You and I,
The sun will shine,
With the sands of time,

You are divine, my sweet lover, it's you I
celebrate,
And you, my sweet lover, inspire my
sovereignty,

You and I,
slow burning bright,
In the sands of time,
You and I,
Two worlds collide,
With the sands of time,
You and I,
Elegantly entwine,
Will you be mine.

A starry night

This starry night,
The universe clear and still,
I am lost but found, in her true beauty,
I am taken by my will,
This journey of love that will shine on through
time,
Two pillars connecting both souls, hearts, and
minds,
Entwining and embracing, as only divine lovers
do,
Authentically devoting, my hearts love shining
through.

First Kiss

First kiss bliss,
Lips on lips,
All smiles and happiness,
The swirls inside,
like those butterflies,
Hands in hands,
embracing worlds,
Enchanting and delicate,
Divine and raw,
2 souls unite,
As sparks ignite,
The flames Of Lasting Love,
and passion like never before.

Morning Mist

5

Early morning, mother moon is still, glowing,
radiant, silent, and full, as she covers the land
with her nourishing Snow White moon mist,
blanketing everyone and everything with her
cool tender kiss, while the world remains
timeless in a peaceful slumber,
The magnificent orange sun, simultaneously
rising steady, and shining so powerful and
brightly, reaching out across the earth, the land,
mother moon, and to all of the darkest places
upon the land. His rays, his sunbeams, melting
into the moons white mystical blanket;
Twas then in that precious moment, the sun and
moon entwined, and gracefully, and without a
whisper, danced together, and were one, in the
blissful, illuminating natural haze, of the dawn
song;
Pure divine warmth, joy, and peace was
embraced, as the mere experience overflowed
the heart and soul, with elegantly lingering
feelings of authenticity, wonderment,
unconditional love and acceptance;
Such a gift for all to be shared.

Dreams

Elegantly she appears to me,
in visions though the night,
Our silhouettes dancing, hand in hand,
under the full moons light,
Authentic, souls naked, beautifully free,
our higher selves sweet play shining through,
A cosmic love, ancient destinies woven, within
the purest dreams of you.

True to Self

7

Through love,
She came into my life,
The Divine Feminine,
Pure Soul Connection,
Destined, cosmic, universal,
Not limited by space nor time,
Higher selves Entwined and United,
complimentary, synchronistic, combined
The Divine Masculine,
When I lived life through love, and true to mine.

Amazing

In our lives things are changing,
I think of you, and see your face shine in my
mind,
Each time with you is amazing,

Holding you close in the morning,
Our warm embrace, I see you through loving
eyes,
I gaze upon you adoring,
This feels amazing,

Day by day, we are growing,
A Leap of love, so beautiful and divine,
Gratefully yours my hearts showing.
This feels amazing,

Inspired by our love,
These words for you, pour sweetly through my
heart my mind,
Love Falling, feels this amazing,
I choose only one,

Thoughts of you, my lady,
All for love,
all for, you and I,

Oh darling this feels amazing.

And as our stories unfolding
Written in the stars, and shining through the
sands of time,
lovers hearts complimenting,
Entwining as one.
This love is amazing.

United dream

In a contented bliss, and grounded knowing,
that they shall re unite, and continue their long
slow, infinite burn for each other,
He embraced her, with his full and pure loving
heart and soul,
holding closely his beloved in a sacred heart
connection,
And when time and space elegantly collided,
he then kissed her sweetly with purpose and
passion,
holding onto this memory,
as if it was there last moment...until they meet
again.

Mother moon

Mother moon, she radiates her luminescent light,
Stars above shine their brightest, in the stillness
of the night,
Glowing aura all around, so silent and profound,
Casting moon beams to all, soft rays of love and
light.

Breaking Free

Observing the chaos this matrix created,
Time and time again in each moment near
deflated,
By society, rules, and laws the powers at be
manipulated,
Taken a world that was never theirs to be taken,
Repeated and reclaimed each part of earth
forsaken,
A price on all things and be punished if you
disobey them,
Still the majority live and believe the lie in fear,
Slaves without a chains in comfortable sedation,
Addicted to the streams and dreams of the
narrative dictated,
While biding my time saving money to buy my
freedom
And live on the land outside their plan as a
sovereign custodian,
As free as one can connected to the earth and the
land and those awake from the corruption,
Filling the souls, cups overflowing with apples
of gold, for all the population.

Lions Gate

13

Walk slowly and purposefully through the Lions
gate,
Experiencing and exploring, this realm to
navigate,
Together and alone, we remain connected,
Divine souls and authentic hearts, one within
ourselves and each-others,
Pure loves true beauty, imperfectly perfected,
Wild and ancient hearts forever young, in no
time and space,
endlessly ours,
Two cups filled and overflowing,
entwined in true lovers vows.

Wet kisses

This night is still, and flashes of light cascade across the sky,
Peaceful feelings wash over me, as the rain gently touches my face,
I embrace them in cosmic bliss, as if they were sweet wet kisses from you, sent in the droplets, just for me,
My soul smiles and my heart melts softly, as I ask a favour to the sky this night,
Please send my acceptance and love with my gratitude in return, to all of you, in this beautiful moment.

Falling

15

Gracefully, falling free and deeply, hand in hand
in silence and knowing, as these authentic souls
merge,
Grounded, two hearts floating in sweet bliss,
entwining into the intrinsic waves and layers of
connection, to the higher selves,
Expectations none, and boundaries defined, as
cosmic lovers embrace in souls rest, here and
now, not limited by space or time,
Times apart, bring pure lovers closer together,
throughout the seasons and changes of each
sunrise, sunset and moon cycles,
Intimately sharing, nature's secrets and wisdom,
the ancient universe of the divine lovers future,
as worlds collide elegantly, with light and love
between two souls, and their cosmic lovers kiss.

With eyes of Love

Looking out through the eyes of love, at the
natural landscapes around me,
I feel connected and at one with the winds,
animals, plants and trees,
I stand grounded and tall, but also still, like a
silent tower of balanced love, darkness and light,
Embracing the overflowing magnificent bliss, in
awe of all things from this life,
A peaceful joy and clarity fills my heart,
with gifts of purity and love,
I breathe it in, I feel its essence with my spirit,
then releasing the energy back to the earth, for
all to experience and love.

Moonlight Ceremony

Sweet mother moon, she slowly rises,
Gracefully above for all to see,
Silently, she casts her beauty upon the earth,
Her feminine magnitude, glowing endlessly,
Her radiantly glowing energy and aura, whispers
softly from above,
To our divine souls, we connect with her and
embrace each other in love,
Though many moons have past us by, this
wonderful mystery,
Now with anticipation and knowing, ready to
shine bright and celebrate,
In our divine love, as two become one, in a
moonlight ceremony.

Whispers

18

There are times when,
even the most subtle of breeze can whisper a
thousand words,
The mystery of the universe shared,
Filling one's heart and soul with a beautiful
flooding of emotions and knowing,
In true essence of the divine.

Summer Rain

The fresh sweet scent of a coming rains
perfume, distinctively fills the air,
Reaching the heavens, and mother earths
atmosphere, on this sacred afternoon,
Gently flowing with love and purpose, the rain
kissing all the earths surface,
Touching the plants, the trees, and all living
things, its purity and aroma, quenching,
rejuvenating, and sustaining, the thirst of all life
itself, with its cascading and beautiful tune,
For one and for all, soaking up all the beautiful
elements divine gifts, as it showers from above,
and to all of us below,
Overflowing and replenished, as the summers
rain passes, and the sun shines bright golden
light upon us all,
With warmth and love, birdsongs abundant, with
joy from above,
An experience for everyone to embrace and
know.

Father and Son

To be a son, To raise one,
To love a son, To Miss one,
To give your all as a father, with no expectations
back,
To stand tall and proud, as he grew into that,
You took the time to nurture, To teach, To guide,
To call,
And know you stand back in silence, as he
teaches you much more,
The challenges in the early years, have
transformed into his capacity now,
This transformation into becoming a man, I sit
back and ponder, wow,
To be a son, To have a son,
To love a son, To raise a son,
I have given you all I know, trust I have in your
heart and soul,
My son it's your journey now.

Directions Tree

The Directions Tree of the Djab Wurrung
people,such a powerful and old a sacred place of
spirituality,
For hundreds of years it has grown, from child's
seed and beyond, now cut down without love
and respect, instantly,
This tree has grown and stood proud and strong,
and past through the generations,
Now removed and been taken, a tribes history
forsaken, as a government uses fear and control,
to push further their limitations,
No heart or no soul, only money and control,
pushing economy, not love, on the population,
The cause and effect of a governments actions
sends ripples of constant devastation,
To the people of this land, let's all unite, hand in
hand, with love and abundant Collective energy,
take back and free our nation,
Authentic sympathies and sorrows go out to
your people, with unconditional love and
respect,
knowing a new seed can be planted, and a new
tree birthed to grow, with the ancient power love
and wisdom of each other's generations.

Beach Bliss

Hello old friend, we meet again, it's been an age
since I bathed in your raw beauty,
With respect I walk gracefully into your depths
and embrace your energies completely,
I feel at home now, finally with you, as my heart
opens and we begin,
My full surrender, and vulnerability with love
and respect, to my soul and your healing within,
I release my self to you and become at peace
with me, expanding my capacity and my love,
entwining with your energies,
Grateful for my transformation as I let go, and
trust your ebb and flow,
supported from your depths, soaking in the
divine and drifting into my glow,
for now I embrace my higher self and soul in
ecstasy,
with the love, knowing and infinite wisdom,
elegantly given by the sea.

Maketh the Man

Tears pour from his eyes and fall softly upon his
face,
As this mountain of a man stands tall and
grateful at the beauty he did create,
Deeply connected he sees his essence all around,
bird song, the earth and trees,
It's time to let go and say goodbye, Now shaken,
now stirred, almost brings him to his knees,
The clarity and wisdom in his eyes knowing that
once all has settled the purity in what's meant to
be will remain,
His sage like ways keep him humbled and
solemn, letting go he endures and sustains,
He walks through this process with
unconditional love, infinite and deep in his heart
and soul,
Embracing his new path and his new future with
the love inner peace and knowing keeping him
whole,
For he travels through life and the earth adapting
with its flow, keeping him on purpose and
through love as only the divine in him doth
know.